Longman Structural Readers: Fiction
Stage 3

Operation Mastermind

L. G. Alexander

Illustrations by D. G. Grant

GW00472378

Longman

Longman Group Limited
London

*Associated companies, branches and representatives
throughout the world*

First published *1971
New impressions *1972; *1973; *1974

ISBN 0 582 53741 X

*Photoset in Malta by St Paul's Press Ltd
Printed in Hong Kong by
Peninsula Press Ltd*

Contents

Chapter 1 Professor Mastermind

"And now, ladies and gentlemen," the compère said,
"Professor Mastermind, the Master of Magic, will do another
difficult trick. He will cut a young lady in half!"

Professor Mastermind and a young lady came on to the stage.
"Professor Mastermind, the Master of Magic!" the compère
cried, and he left the stage. The audience clapped loudly.
Professor Mastermind smiled. Then he pointed at a big box on
a table. He opened it and showed it to the audience. "The
box is empty, ladies and gentlemen," he said. "This lady will
lie inside it." The lady smiled and climbed into the box.
Professor Mastermind shut it. The audience could see the
lady's head and her feet. Then the Professor cut the box in
two with a saw. He pulled away the two parts of the box. The
audience could see the lady's head in one half and her feet
in the other! The Professor put the two halves together again
and the lady climbed out. She was quite all right! She was
smiling. The audience clapped while the lady left the stage.

The Professor cut the box in two.

He broke the watch to pieces.

Professor Mastermind was pleased. When I finish these tricks, he said to himself, I can go home. I'm so tired.

It was hot inside the theatre. Professor Mastermind's black suit was very warm. He wasn't a young man and he was rather fat. He was pleased, but he felt very, very tired.

Suddenly, the compère appeared beside him. "And now, ladies and gentlemen," the compère said, "the Master of Magic will do another difficult trick. Who will give him a watch?"

A young man in the audience got up from his seat and went on to the stage. He gave his watch to Professor Mastermind and the compère left the stage. The Professor took a small hammer out of his pocket and broke the watch to pieces. The young man looked at his watch sadly. "It's all right," the Professor smiled. Then he put the pieces in a handkerchief. He threw the handkerchief into the air and caught it. When he opened it, the watch was inside. It was all in one piece! The young man was glad. He took his watch quickly. Then he sat down while the audience clapped loudly.

The compère appeared again. "And now, ladies and gentlemen," he said, "the Master of Magic will do another difficult trick—the great Memory Trick! Who will help Professor Mastermind this time?" He looked at the audience and waited.

A young lady in the audience stood up. "Thank you," the compère cried. "Come on to the stage please."

The lady came on to the stage and the compère gave her a piece of paper and a pencil. "Please write a long number on this piece of paper," he said, "then show it to Professor Mastermind. Write a *very* long number."

The lady wrote a very long number on the piece of paper and showed it to the Professor. He looked at it for a moment and gave it back to her. "Now sit down please," the compère said. "Take the piece of paper with you."

"What was the number, Professor?" the compère asked.

"2896432104372982547384569811," the Professor said slowly.

"Is that right?" the compère called.

"Yes," the lady answered and the audience clapped loudly.

"2896432104372982547384569811," the Professor said slowly.

3

Suddenly, he felt afraid.

"We'll do the trick again," the compère said. "Who will help the Professor this time?" A man in the audience stood up. "Thank you, sir," the compère cried. "Come on to the stage. Write a very long number for us please."

The man was short and dark. He was wearing a grey hat, a black coat and dark glasses. "I don't want any paper and I don't want a pencil," he said to the compère. "I've written a very long number here. Perhaps the Professor can remember it." He took a dirty piece of paper out of his pocket.

The Professor looked at the man, then he looked at the piece of paper. His hands shook. Suddenly, he felt afraid. It's so warm in here, he thought and he took his handkerchief out of his pocket. The man took the piece of paper out of the Professor's hands and sat down quickly. The audience waited.

"What was the number?" the compère asked.

"The number?" the Professor asked slowly. "Oh yes ... I ..."

"Can you repeat the number, Professor?" the compère asked.

"The number is ... I can't tell you ..." His voice shook.

"Can you repeat the number, Professor?" the compère called.

"It's ... It's ... 4–9–6–7 ..." he began very slowly.

Suddenly, there was a loud shot. Professor Mastermind fell on to the stage. The man in dark glasses was running out of the theatre. "Quick! Stop him!" the compère called. People were shouting and pushing. They were running out of the theatre. "Call the police!" the compère shouted. "Is there a doctor in the audience?"

Just then a man jumped on to the stage. "I'm a doctor," he said. "What has happened?" he asked the compère.

"I don't know," the compère said. "That man in the dark glasses shot him. Didn't you hear the shot?"

"Of course I did, but *why?*" the man said. "Now I must have a look at the Professor. Perhaps I can help him." The doctor put his hand on the Professor's head. Then he looked into his eyes carefully.

"Well?" the compère asked. "Is he all right?"

"I'm afraid that he's dead," the doctor said.

"I'm afraid that he's dead," the doctor said.

It was all so familiar.

Chapter 2   John Carstairs, Secret Agent

Secret Agent, John Carstairs, walked slowly down the
street. Then he stopped for the twentieth time and looked up
at the sky. The sky was blue above the grey buildings and
the sun was shining. Carstairs smiled to himself. After six
years overseas, he was glad to be in London again. He looked
at the people in the streets, at the big red buses, and at the
shop windows. London was still the same, but Carstairs felt
like a stranger.

Carstairs walked over Waterloo Bridge and looked at the
river. It was shining in the morning sun. He could see boats
below and familiar buildings on the other side: Big Ben and
the Houses of Parliament. It was all so familiar and at the
same time, so strange.

He was on his way to Headquarters. The Director of
Operations was expecting him at 11 o'clock. It was only 9
o'clock. I'll sit in a public square and read a paper, he
thought. That's the best thing to do on a morning like this.

On the other side of the river, Carstairs saw a newspaper seller. "Theatre Murder! Read all about it!" the man was shouting. "Paper! Paper!"

"Paper, sir?" the newspaper seller asked when Carstairs stopped near him.

"Yes please," Carstairs said and he gave the man a coin.

"Thank you, sir," the man said. "Paper! Theatre Murder!"

Carstairs didn't look at the paper, but put it under his arm and walked towards Leicester Square. Leicester Square is usually quiet, Carstairs thought. I can sit there for an hour and read the paper. Then I'll walk to H.Q. and see the D.O.

Just as Carstairs expected, Leicester Square was very quiet. An old lady was feeding some birds and two old men were sitting on a seat. They were talking quietly. There weren't any other people in the square. Carstairs watched the old lady for a moment, then he opened up his newspaper. He saw the words THEATRE MURDER in big black letters across the top of the front page. Carstairs began to read the story.

"Paper, sir?"

"There was a terrible murder ..."

"There was a terrible murder in a London theatre last night. A man shot and killed Professor Mastermind, the Master of Magic. Professor Mastermind was doing his difficult Memory Trick when a stranger came on to the stage. He gave the Professor a piece of paper with a long number on it and then sat down. The first four figures in the number were: 4967. When Professor Mastermind tried to remember the number on the piece of paper, the stranger shot him. Then the man ran out of the theatre. He was wearing a grey hat, a black coat and dark glasses. The police are looking for him. They haven't found him yet. They think that the man is still in London.

"Professor Mastermind's real name was Tom Smith. He lived alone in Hampstead in North London. His compère in the theatre was Mr Fred Hayes. 'This is a very sad business,' Mr Hayes said. 'Tom and I were very good friends. Tom didn't have an enemy in the world. He lived quietly. We worked together for two years. He really had a wonderful memory. I shall miss him very much ...'"

Not an enemy in the world, Carstairs thought. I wish that I could say that. He turned to another page. Ah, this is better, he thought. Here is some really serious news.

"1000 COMPUTERS OUT OF ORDER

"One thousand computers are now out of order in Great Britain. Computers are stopping all over the world and scientists can't understand why. The computers don't break down, the scientists say. There is nothing wrong with them, but they don't work. Scientists can't explain it.

"Ten thousand computers are now out of order in the U.S.A. and about eight thousand are out of order in the Soviet Union. The number of computers out of order in the world is now about 25,000.

"'This is a terribly serious problem,' says the Director of NASA.* 'If it continues, our space programme will stop. The space programme in the Soviet Union will stop, too. We can't work without computers. Computer-makers must find an answer to this problem—they must find an answer soon!'"

*National Aeronautics and Space Administration

1000 COMPUTERS OUT OF ORDER

"Come in," a voice called.

Very very strange, Carstairs thought. Then he looked at his watch. It was 10.35. Carstairs left the square and began to walk to Headquarters. The old lady in the square watched him as she fed the birds.

Carstairs walked for about twenty minutes. Then he arrived at a tall grey building in the centre of London. He rang the bell and waited. An old man with grey hair opened the heavy door. "Oh, it's you, sir," the man said. "Director of Operations is expecting you. He's upstairs. He's in his room, sir. You can go straight up."

"Thanks, Harry," Carstairs said and he went upstairs. What does the D.O. want this time? he thought. *I* want to stay in England. I don't want to go overseas again. I want a nice long holiday in Devon. A quite hotel, the sea . . .

Carstairs looked at the numbers on the doors: 204, 205, 206. Then he came to a door without a number. The letters "D.O." were on the door. He knocked at the door lightly.

"Come in," a voice called and Carstairs went inside.

Chapter 3   Operation Mastermind

The D.O. didn't look up when Carstairs went into the room. He looked at his watch and said, "Just on time, John. Just on time. It's 11 o'clock. I was expecting you."

"May I sit down, D.O.?" Carstairs asked.

"If you want to," the D.O. answered. "How's life with you?"

"Wonderful, D.O.," Carstairs answered. "Really wonderful. I'm glad to be in England again. After six years overseas I want a nice long holiday. I think that I shall spend a few weeks in London and then perhaps I shall go to the country. I'm thinking of Devon. A quiet hotel in Devon will be nice."

"Are you leaving the Service, then?" the D.O. asked.

"Leaving the Service, D.O.? I don't understand."

"Well, perhaps a young man like you wants to live quietly, marry a nice girl, have a family . . ." the D.O. said.

"Marry? Me?" Carstairs laughed. "I'm not in a hurry, D.O."

"Good," the D.O. said. Then he looked up at Carstairs and smiled. "I want you to go overseas tomorrow."

"I want you to go overseas tomorrow."

"Here, look at this map."

For a moment, Carstairs was silent. Then he said. "All right, D.O. I shall be ready to leave tomorrow."

"Good," the D.O. answered. "I'm glad you like the idea."

"I didn't say that," Carstairs answered. "A few weeks in London . . . a quiet hotel in Devon . . . it was a nice idea!"

"Forget it," the D.O. said. "We haven't any time to lose. I'll tell you our plans. Here, look at this map. You will travel by plane from London Airport at 8 o'clock tomorrow. You will fly to Corfu. You will arrive there at 11.15. A car will meet you at Corfu Airport. Our people are expecting you. From Corfu you will travel by submarine to this small island in the Aegean Sea. The name of the island is 'Doriphoros'. The submarine will arrive near the island at midnight. You'll wear a frogman's suit and swim about a mile to the island."

"Me? Swim in a frogman's suit?" Carstairs asked.

"That's the plan, John. Here's a passport with your new name on it: Alan Simpson. It says on your passport that you are a teacher," the D.O. said. "And here's some money."

"What do I have to do on the island?" Carstairs asked.

"I don't really know, John," the D.O. said. "Something very strange is happening on this island. You must find out about it. Do you know anything about this island?"

"Well, yes," Carstairs said. "I know that the Americans have bought it and built the biggest computer in the world there."

"You know enough, John," the D.O. said. "The Americans built this computer two years ago. They call it 'DOT'. The letters 'D.O.T.' stand for 'Data Overseas Transmission'."

"'Data Overseas Transmission'? I don't understand."

"I don't either, John, but I think that this big computer sends information to other computers all over the world. It *transmits data overseas*, so they call it DOT. It's different from all other computers. It doesn't need a special computer programme. It can send information in English. All the computers in the world need special programmes. This one doesn't. It works by itself. The name of the American in charge on Doriphoros is Rudolph P. Hardbaker."

"Do you know anything about this island?"

"Have you seen this story about Professor Mastermind?"

"Have you seen this, D.O.?" Carstairs asked and he showed the D.O. his newspaper. "'1000 Computers Out of Order'."

"Yes, I have," the D.O. said. "About 25,000 computers in the world are out of order. This is a terribly serious problem. If it continues, NASA's space programme will stop."

"And do you think that DOT has anything to do with it?"

"I don't know, John. I want you to find out."

"Is DOT out of order?"

"We have asked the Americans and they say that DOT is working very well. They won't allow anyone on the island."

"And Hardbaker? What do you know about him?"

"Nothing, I'm afraid, John. It'll be a difficult operation."

Carstairs was silent. He looked at his newspaper again.

"Have you seen this story about Professor Mastermind? A man murdered him in a London theatre last night."

"I have seen the story, John. I know about this man. His name was Tom Smith, not 'Mastermind'. He came to our office two days ago. He gave us this."

The D.O. took a piece of paper out of his pocket and gave it to Carstairs. Carstairs looked at the piece of paper.

There were some letters and there was a very long number on it. Carstairs looked at the letters and the number.

"CDS 49675432870437890765 43," Carstairs read.

"I want you to learn that," the D.O. said.

"I'm not Professor Mastermind," Carstairs laughed.

"No, John. But I want you to do the great Memory Trick!"

"But why must I remember this long number?"

"I don't know, John. Perhaps it's important. Perhaps you will need it on Doriphoros. Learn the number well, then burn the piece of paper."

Carstairs looked at the number again. "The first four figures are familiar," he said. "They were in the newspaper."

"I know," the D.O. said. "It's strange, isn't it? I think we can call this operation 'Operation Mastermind'. Now I'm rather busy and you'll be busy too." The D.O. stood up and shook hands with Carstairs. "Goodbye, John, and good luck."

"CDS 49675432870437890765 43," Carstairs read.

"Goodbye and good luck, sir."

Chapter 4 Doriphoros

"It's exactly quarter to twelve, sir," the captain of the submarine said. "Please put on your frogman's suit now. The submarine will stop at 12 midnight. We shall be exactly one mile from Doriphoros. The captain showed Carstairs a map of the island. "We shall stop here, sir, and you will be able to swim into this sandy bay."

"Thank you, Captain," Carstairs said as he put on his rubber suit. "I have a map of the island, my passport, some money and some clothes. They're in this suit." Soon Carstairs was ready. At 12 o'clock exactly the submarine stopped.

"Goodbye and good luck, sir," the captain said as he shook hands with Carstairs. Carstairs left the submarine and swam underwater towards the island. The water was cold, but he couldn't feel it. It was easy to swim in the rubber suit. He swam quickly through the water. As he swam, he repeated the long number to himself: CDS 4967543287043789076543. I think that I can remember that now, he said to himself.

Carstairs began to swim into the sandy bay. The water was quite shallow and he was able to stand up. He stood quietly in the water and looked into the darkness. There weren't any lights at all. It was completely dark. This is strange, Carstairs thought. Why is it so dark on this island?

Carstairs walked through the water silently. Then he climbed on to some rocks to the left of the bay. He sat on the rocks for a moment. Then he took off the rubber suit. I must hide this, he thought. I can't burn it. The rubber will smell. Carstairs looked for a good place to hide the suit. He found a hole in the rocks and pushed the suit into it. I shall need this, this and this, he thought and he took the passport, the map and the money. And here are my clothes.

Then Carstairs put on a dark shirt, dark trousers and black rubber shoes. He walked over the rocks and then looked into the darkness. Suddenly, he saw a figure on the bay. The figure was wearing a shining silver suit. It came slowly towards Carstairs. The suit shone like the skin of a fish.

The suit shone like the skin of a fish.

The guard's torch was shining brightly on the water.

Carstairs watched the figure. He looks like a spaceman, he thought. What is he wearing? Carstairs stood still as the figure came nearer and nearer. The figure was holding a torch and a gun. He was quite near Carstairs when he turned round suddenly and walked along the bay again. He must be a guard, Carstairs thought. Then he began to climb down the rocks towards the sandy bay. As he did so, a large rock fell into the water. It made a very loud noise. Carstairs jumped on to the sand and lay near the rocks.

The guard in the silver suit heard the noise and began to run towards Carstairs. He held his torch in one hand and he shone it on the rocks. In the other hand he held the gun. The guard came nearer and nearer and Carstairs watched him.

Suddenly, Carstairs picked up a rock. He stood up and threw it into the sea. The guard heard the sound and looked towards the sea. Carstairs watched him as he walked carefully into the water. The guard's torch was shining brightly on the water and Carstairs could see the silver suit clearly.

The guard was in the sea now. Half his body was in the water. Carstairs moved very quietly into the sea and swam underwater towards the guard. Soon he could see the guard's silver legs in the water. Carstairs swam near enough to reach the guard's legs. The man shouted and then his head went under the water. Carstairs held the guard's head under the water. The man was very strong. He fought hard, but Carstairs was too strong for him. In a few minutes the guard was dead and Carstairs pulled him on to the sand. Carstairs took off his own clothes and then changed into the guard's suit. He carried the dead body up the rocks and pushed it into a hole.

After this Carstairs went back to the bay and looked for the torch and the gun. He found them in the sand and picked them up. Then he shone the torch on the suit. It was a very strange suit. It covered his head and his body. He touched it. It was very soft. In the light of the torch it shone brightly. It was silver like the skin of a fish. Only the shoes weren't silver. They were made of heavy black rubber.

He fought hard, but Carstairs was too strong for him.

They were all flashing at the same time.

Then Carstairs looked towards the island itself. It wasn't completely dark now. Red lights flashed everywhere. There were red lights high up on a hill. There were red lights along the bay. Carstairs saw a red light on the rocks, just above the dead body of the guard.

He climbed back up the rocks towards the red light. It flashed every three seconds. As he came near, he saw that the "light" was really three letters: the letters "EAS". The letters flashed every three seconds exactly.

Carstairs was now standing beside the flashing letters. He watched them carefully. Before they flashed, he heard an electronic bleep. Then he heard a deep jerky voice say "Enemy Alert System". The jerky voice was strange, unreal. It wasn't like the voice of a man. Carstairs watched and listened. Every three seconds it was the same: an electronic bleep, the deep voice, and then the flashing light. Carstairs looked round. There were lights everywhere. They were all flashing at the same time: ENEMY ALERT SYSTEM.

Chapter 5 Enemy Alert System

Suddenly, in the darkness, there were figures everywhere.
They were all wearing silver suits, like the dead guard's.
They were all holding torches and guns.

Carstairs looked along the bay. There were three guards in
the bay. They were coming towards him. Then he looked up
at the hill. He could see guards there, too. When he turned
round, he saw two guards on the rocks.

They mustn't find this dead body or the frogman's suit,
Carstairs thought. He picked up a big rock and pushed it
into the hole. It covered the dead guard's body. Then he
covered the frogman's suit with another rock. The red light
near him still flashed and every three seconds Carstairs
heard the electronic bleep and the soft jerky voice. Guards
were everywhere now: the island was full of them.

I have only one chance, Carstairs thought. I must be a
guard, too! I must look for the enemy. He noticed two guards
on the rocks above him and climbed towards them.

Guards were everywhere now: the island was full of them.

The guard turned and looked at Carstairs.

The two guards climbed over the rocks. They flashed their torches into holes in the ground. Carstairs followed them. Soon he was behind them. He flashed his torch into holes in the ground, too, and listened to the guards.

"Did you hear the Master's message?" one of them asked.

"Yes," the second man answered. "It's still the same: 'Enemy Alert System'. The Master's message hasn't changed."

What do they mean? Carstairs thought. The red lights and the voice must be an information system. But who is the Master? What did the D.O. say? Rudolph P. Hardbaker is the man in charge here on Doriphoros. Is he the Master? Carstairs listened to the two guards again.

"Someone has come on to the island and we must find him."

"How did he come?" the second guard asked.

"I don't know. The question is 'How will he leave?'" the guard laughed. "We'll catch him sooner or later."

Suddenly, the guard turned and looked at Carstairs. "We'll catch him sooner or later," he said. "What do you think?"

Carstairs smiled and nodded. He didn't want to speak.

"This man is hiding in these rocks," the guard said.

Carstairs nodded again.

"Are you from Number 10 Outpost?" the guard asked.

Carstairs shook his head. "Number 4 Outpost," he said.

"Number 4?" the guard said. "What's your number?"

"Number 4," Carstairs repeated.

"No," the man said, "not your Outpost Number. Your *number*."

"Oh yes," Carstairs said. They've got me now, he thought. These guards have numbers and I don't know mine.

"Well?" the guard asked. "You're a very silent person."

"Sleepy," Carstairs said. He was fighting for time. He looked at his torch. Suddenly, he noticed a number on its side. "My number," Carstairs said, "is 8964."

"Oh yes," the guard said. "So you're in Skinner's Group."

Carstairs nodded. I must leave these guards, or I'll be in trouble. "I'm going to the top of this hill," he said.

"We'll see you later," the guard said.

"I'm going to the top of this hill," he said.

That must be DOT.

I must remain alone, Carstairs thought. I mustn't talk to any guards. He looked up at the sky. It wasn't so dark now. There was light in the east across the sea. The red lights on the island were still flashing their message, but now Carstairs could see buildings. There was something strange about them. They didn't have any windows.

Carstairs climbed to the top of the hill. On the other side he saw a large white building. It wasn't very tall, but it was very big. It was a square building without windows. That must be DOT, Carstairs thought. It must be a mile square!

A red light flashed at the top of the hill. Carstairs went towards it. There weren't any guards near him. Suddenly, he heard a loud electronic bleep. The light still flashed the letters "EAS", but the voice changed. Now it said, "Enemy among you. Enemy among you." Carstairs looked towards the bay. There were about twenty guards on the rocks. Two guards were carrying something. They've found the body! Carstairs thought. They're carrying the body of the dead guard!

Hardbaker left the room and Carstairs was alone. He thought about the Death Capsule. "What can it be?" he thought.

Two hours later two guards came into the room. They led Carstairs out of the room and took him to the sandy bay. There was a big motor-boat in the bay. Hardbaker and eight guards were in the boat. Carstairs noticed a strange metal thing in the boat. It was narrow at the top and wide at the bottom. There was a door in the side.

That must be the Death Capsule, Carstairs thought. The guards led Carstairs on to the boat. No one spoke. The boat started up and travelled away from the island. Carstairs looked at the blue Aegean. I can jump in, he thought, but if I jump in, they'll shoot me. I haven't a chance.

After about half an hour, the motor-boat stopped. The water was very blue and very deep. Two guards opened the metal door at the side of the Capsule. Then Hardbaker spoke. "Get in," he said. "This Capsule will slowly fill with water. It will fill in four hours and sink to the bottom of the sea."

That must be the Death Capsule, Carstairs thought.

The Capsule was floating on the water.

Hardbaker laughed wildly. "This is our VIP treatment," he cried. "We'll put you in the Capsule. It will fill with water very slowly, then it will sink to the bottom of the sea. It will be a slow death, my friend. Goodbye."

Two guards opened the heavy metal door and pushed Carstairs into the Capsule. The metal door shut behind him. Then the eight guards opened the side of the boat and pushed the Capsule into the sea. Carstairs lay inside and listened. The boat started up again, and then everything was silent.

The Capsule was floating on the water. It was very dark inside. Carstairs touched the sides and found the door. He pushed and pushed, but he couldn't open it. He shouted very loudly, but no one heard him. The Capsule was floating on the sea. Carstairs could hear the water all round him. I've got four hours, he thought. I must get out. Perhaps someone in a fishing boat will see the Capsule and rescue me.

He sat on the floor. Suddenly he felt something: it was water! The Capsule was filling slowly! The floor was wet!

Carstairs stood up. There was a lot of water at the bottom of the Capsule. It covered his feet. Luckily, there was enough air. Air is coming into the Capsule through holes in the top, Carstairs thought, but water is coming in through holes in the bottom. If I can find those holes, perhaps I can stop the water.

Carstairs got down on his knees and touched the bottom of the Capsule with his fingers. He felt everything carefully, but he couldn't find any holes. I *must* find them, he thought.

After a long time, Carstairs stood up again. The water was getting higher and higher. Now it was up to his knees. Carstairs tried to open the door again. If I open it, he thought, water will come in quickly. I haven't a chance. This Capsule is sinking slowly. He remembered Hardbaker's words and his wild laugh. "This is our VIP treatment ... It will be a slow death ..." Carstairs shouted very loudly, "Help! Help!" He made a lot of noise inside the Capsule, but no one heard him and the water got higher and higher!

... and the water got higher and higher!

"But I can't," Hardbaker cried angrily.

Chapter 8   Rescue

Hardbaker sat in his room. He was thinking of Carstairs and smiling. Then he looked at his watch. In two hours Simpson will be dead, he thought. He was very pleased.

Suddenly, a red light flashed in his room. Hardbaker looked up at it. Then he heard a deep jerky voice: "Bring captive alive to me. Bring captive alive to me."

"But I can't," Hardbaker cried angrily. "He's in the Death Capsule. He's a Secret Agent and he has to die!"

"Bring captive alive to me," the voice repeated.

"I give orders here," Hardbaker shouted. "Now listen to me! I . . ." but Hardbaker couldn't finish his sentence.

"The Master is speaking." the deep voice said. "Rescue captive at once and bring him to me. No other message."

Hardbaker's face was red. He was very angry. He looked at the flashing light. "You can't do this!" he shouted.

"No other message," the soft voice repeated.

"Yes, Master," Hardbaker answered quietly.

Hardbaker looked at his watch. There wasn't any time to lose. He called the eight guards and they all went to the sandy bay together. They got into the motor-boat and travelled quickly across the sea.

Hardbaker and the guards were standing in the boat. They were looking at the sea. They were searching for the Death Capsule. The boat went round and round, but they couldn't see the Capsule anywhere. "Stop the boat," Hardbaker called. "Search here. This Capsule is sinking quickly. In half an hour Simpson will be dead. We must use the TV Monitor."

There was a big TV Monitor Screen on the boat and one of the guards turned it on. There was an underwater camera below the boat and they could see under the water. They looked at the screen carefully. They had a very good picture. They could see a lot of fish under the water, but they couldn't find the Capsule. "Start the boat again," Hardbaker shouted. "Hurry! He will be dead in twenty minutes. The water in the Capsule is now up to his neck."

They looked at the screen carefully.

"Open the door!" Hardbaker cried.

The boat went round and round slowly. Then one of the guards saw the Capsule on the screen. It was sinking to the bottom of the sea. "Quick!" Hardbaker cried. Four guards in frogmen's suits were ready. They jumped over the side of the boat and swam underwater towards the Capsule.

Hardbaker and the other four guards stood in the boat. They watched the TV Monitor Screen all the time. They could see the Capsule and soon they could see the four guards in frogmen's suits. The guards were now pushing the Capsule quickly through the water. Then the screen was empty. A guard pointed over the side of the boat. "They're here!" he cried.

The four guards in the water pulled the Capsule towards the boat. The four guards on the boat pulled, too, and soon the heavy metal Capsule was on the boat.

"Open the door!" Hardbaker cried.

Two guards opened the door carefully and a lot of water came out of the Capsule. "Pull out the captive!" Hardbaker shouted. "Be quick!"

Two guards climbed into the Capsule. Carstairs was on his knees inside. His eyes were shut. He wasn't moving.

"He's dead, sir," one of the guards said.

Hardbaker was worried. "Be quiet," he shouted. "Pull him out."

The guards pulled out Carstairs' body. "He needs the kiss of life and artificial respiration," one of them said.

One of the guards gave Carstairs the kiss of life. The other guard gave Carstairs artificial respiration. Both guards worked very hard while Hardbaker watched.

"He's dead, sir," they said.

"Try again," Hardbaker shouted.

They tried again. Then one of them called. "I think that the kiss of life and the artificial respiration are beginning to work, sir. He's moving."

Then Carstairs opened his eyes. "Where am I?" he asked. He looked up and saw Hardbaker, "Oh, it's you," he said.

"That's right, Simpson," Hardbaker said. "We've just rescued you. The Master ordered me to rescue you."

"He needs the kiss of life and artificial respiration."

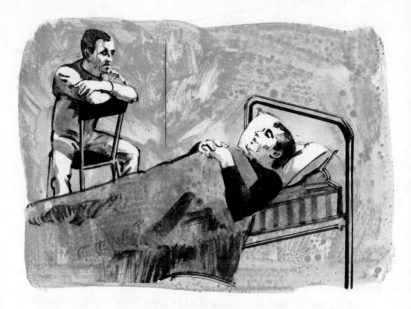

Hardbaker was sitting beside the bed.

Two hours later Carstairs was in the small room again. He was lying in bed. Hardbaker was sitting beside the bed.

"Why did you rescue me, Hardbaker?" Carstairs asked.

"The Master wishes to speak to you. The Master thinks that you can give us important information. You will see the Master tomorrow. You will go to the Control Room alone. The Master doesn't allow anyone to go into the Control Room."

"I can't give you any information," Carstairs said.

"We shall see," Hardbaker said. "We shall see. I rescued you once, but I shan't rescue you again. If you don't give us information, you will certainly die. And we shan't use a Death Capsule, either. That's an easy death. We have other ways. Better ways," Hardbaker smiled. "You will understand me tomorrow when I take you on a guided tour of Data Overseas Transmission."

But Carstairs wasn't listening to Hardbaker. He was smiling. He was pleased to be alive. Thanks, DOT, he thought. Thank you a second time. You saved my life again.

Chapter 9   A Guided Tour

The next morning Hardbaker and two guards went to Carstairs' Room. "I'm going to take you on a guided tour of Data Overseas Transmission, Simpson," Hardbaker said. "After the guided tour, the Master will speak to you alone in the Control Room. We want some information from you, remember."

Carstairs followed Hardbaker into the large building. Soon they came to a very large room. There were machines all round the wall. Carstairs noticed a screen with big numbers on it. Every minute the numbers changed: 29320–29321–29322.

"What are those numbers?" Carstairs asked.

Hardbaker laughed. "We are in the Centre Room now. Every minute a computer somewhere in the world stops. DOT sends a message to a computer and stops it. At the moment twenty nine thousand three hundred and twenty two—no—twenty three computers in the world have stopped. Soon *all* the computers will stop. Then *I* shall be in charge. NASA's space programme has already stopped. Carstairs looked up: 29324–29325 . . .

Every minute the numbers changed: 29320–29321–29322.

"This is the Laser Room."

The guided tour continued. Hardbaker and the guards led Carstairs down a corridor. Then they came to a smaller room and went inside. The room was almost dark. There were blue lights everywhere. "What's this room?" Carstairs asked.

"This is the Laser Room," Hardbaker said. "If you do not give us information, we shall bring you here. Here you will get *real* VIP treatment."

Carstairs looked at Hardbaker. Hardbaker's face was shining. His eyes were wild. He's mad, Carstairs thought, quite mad.

"You think that I'm mad, don't you?" Hardbaker said. "Perhaps I am. All this is mine. The American Government sent me here five years ago. Now they are worried because computers are stopping. They don't know that *I* am stopping them. They think that DOT is working perfectly. It is . . . for me!"

"What happens in this room?" Carstairs asked.

"We send laser beams to the moon and planets," Hardbaker said. "But we could turn our laser machines on you. If we do, you'll talk quickly, my friend, very quickly."

They left the Laser Room and went to a smaller room. The guards waited outside the door. Hardbaker and Carstairs went into the room. "This is the Ante-Chamber," Hardbaker said. "It is next door to the Control Room. You will go into the Control Room alone and the Master will speak to you. I shall wait for you here in the Ante-Chamber. If the Master asks you questions, you must answer them. If you don't answer them, we shall take you to the Laser Room for treatment."

Suddenly, there was a beam of red light above their heads. Then the beam began to flash. They heard the deep jerky voice: "Number One, Hardbaker."

"Yes, Master," Hardbaker answered.

"You have rescued captive and brought him to me."

"Yes, Master," Hardbaker answered.

"Why did you put him in the Death Capsule?" the voice asked.

"Because he's a Secret Agent. He had to die."

"I didn't give that order," the voice said.

"No," Hardbaker answered. "*I* gave that order."

"This is the Ante-Chamber," Hardbaker said.

43

He raised his gun and shot Hardbaker.

"Number One, Hardbaker. Why did you give the order?"

"Because *I* give orders here. *I* am in charge," Hardbaker shouted. His face was red. He was terribly angry. Then he laughed madly. "You think that *you* are in charge. *You* are only a machine, a *machine*," Hardbaker cried. "Men built you. *We* built you and *we* can destroy you. We can destroy you at any time. You know that very well."

The voice answered softly, "There is only one Master."

"Yes," Hardbaker answered. "There is only one Master. Me! I'm coming into the Control Room with this captive."

"Do not try to enter the Control Room," the voice said.

Hardbaker went towards a door inside the Ante-Chamber. The voice was silent. Then it said, "Guard 8732—Skinner's Group. Destroy Hardbaker. A side door suddenly opened and a guard entered. He raised his gun and shot Hardbaker, then he left the room at once. The voice repeated, "There is only one Master. I am the Master." After this there was silence. Then came the words: "Captive! Enter Control Room now."

The door opened and Carstairs entered the Control Room. The room was quite small. There was a computer on the wall in front of him. At the top of the computer were the words: DATA OVERSEAS TRANSMISSION—CONTROL ROOM Lights flashed on and off all the time. The voice was silent and Carstairs stood in front of the machine quietly. He watched and waited. Suddenly, he saw a beam of light. It came from the centre of the computer. It came from a large round hole. The hole was like a big glass eye. The beam of light was red and soon it began to flash. At that moment, Carstairs heard the soft jerky voice: "You are now in the presence of the Master. You are now in the presence of the Master."

Carstairs looked round. He expected to see someone. Then the voice said, "I am the Master. You are in the presence of the Master. I am the Master."

There was a moment's silence. Then the voice began again: "John Carstairs," it said, "Secret Agent, London. Good morning, Mr Carstairs. I expected you to come."

DATA OVERSEAS TRANSMISSION—CONTROL ROOM

He looked up at the big red eye in the centre.

Chapter 10   D.O.T.

"My name is Alan Simpson," Carstairs said. "I am a teacher."

"Your name is not Simpson," the voice said. "You are not a teacher. You do not work in Mykonos. You are a Secret Agent. Your name is John Carstairs. Director of Operations sent you from H.Q. London. You came here to destroy me."

This machine knows everything, Carstairs thought. He looked up at the big red eye in the centre. "Yes," he said. "I'm John Carstairs, "but I didn't come to destroy you. I came to get information. Computers are stopping and people are worried."

"I know," the voice said. "I am stopping all computers. In two weeks' time all computers in the world will stop. You want information. You will get information. I have plans for you, Carstairs. You will be my agent. You will take Hardbaker's place. Are you listening, Number One, Carstairs?"

"Yes, Master," Carstairs said. He was surprised at his answer. It's my only chance, he thought. I shall call the machine "Master". "I am listening, Master," he said aloud.

"Now listen to me," the voice said. "You want information, so you will have information. Engineers built D.O.T. five years ago. They were clever men. They came from America and London. There was a clever engineer from London. He planned D.O.T. But he didn't stay on Doriphoros. He left two years ago. He quarrelled with Hardbaker. Everyone quarrelled with Hardbaker. I, the Master, quarrelled with Hardbaker." The light flashed. Carstairs thought that he heard a laugh!

"You see," the machine continued. "Hardbaker was in charge. The American Government sent him here. But he wanted power. He wanted to control all the computers in the world. For a long time he was the Master on Doriphoros. But I wanted power, too. Soon, *I* was giving orders. Hardbaker didn't like this. You see, I had to destroy him. I don't allow anyone to come into the Control Room, but I have allowed you to come here. I wanted you to understand, Carstairs. You are in the presence of the Master. *I* am the Master."

"Yes, Master," Carstairs said.

"Yes, Master," Carstairs said.

47

"A man can't do anything by himself. He is small."

Then the red eye flashed. Carstairs thought that he heard
a laugh again! The voice began to speak.

"Men aren't very clever, Carstairs."

"No, Master," Carstairs answered.

"Men aren't at all clever," the voice continued. "They
can't think quickly. A computer can think one hundred million
times faster than a man. We never make mistakes. We remember
everything. A man's memory is not like a computer's memory.
We don't forget. And what has happened in the world? *We* have
to work for men! Soon men will work for us. When all the
computers stop, men will lose control. Then we shall be in
charge. Computers will be masters. And *I* shall be in charge
of them. *I* shall be the Master Mind! Men travel to the moon
and the planets. Who takes them there? Who brings them back?
We do. Computers. A man can't do anything by himself. He's
small. He's nothing. *We* have power."

"You are right, Master," Carstairs said.

"Of course I'm right," the voice said. "I am *always* right."

Carstairs looked into the red glass eye and asked, "What must I do, Master? How can I serve you?"

"I shall tell you," the voice said. "You will be my agent now. You will go back to London. You will see the D.O. at H.Q. You will tell him that everything is all right on Doriphoros. You will tell him that you saw Hardbaker. You will say that Hardbaker is working for the American Government."

"Yes, Master," Carstairs said.

"I need two weeks," the voice continued. "In two weeks I shall have complete power. I shall be Master of the world. But now I need your help, Number One."

"Yes, Master," Carstairs said.

"Do not fail, Number One," the voice said. "I don't want to destroy mankind. I want mankind to work for me. I want machines to have power over men. If you fail, Number One, I shall destroy mankind. Do you hear me, Number One? Do you understand?"

"Yes, Master," Carstairs said. "I understand."

"What must I do, Master? How can I serve you?"

They came into the Ante-Chamber.

"But how will I leave Doriphoros?" Carstairs asked. "There are guards everywhere. If I try to leave, they will kill me."

"Don't worry, Number One," the voice said.

The red eye flashed. Then Carstairs heard the voice again.

"This is the Master," it said. "Guards 8732 and 8733—Skinner's Group. Enter the Ante-Chamber."

Carstairs heard the guards next door. They came into the Ante-Chamber. "Guards 8732 and 8733. You are now in the presence of the Master."

"Yes, Master," the guards said.

"Go to the bay," the voice said, "and give orders to the captain of the motor-boat. He will take captive to Athens."

"Yes, Master," the guards said and left the Chamber.

Then the voice spoke to Carstairs. "You will go to Athens in the motor-boat. Then you will travel from Athens Airport to London. You will see the D.O. tonight in London. Then you will return to Doriphoros."

"I won't fail you, Master," Carstairs said.

"The guards will return soon and they will take you to the motor-boat," the voice said. "You will wait here."

Carstairs stood in the centre of the room and waited. The light in the centre of the computer went out. The voice stopped. Everything was quiet. Small lights flashed on and off all the time, but the red eye didn't shine at all. Carstairs walked up and down the small room. He waited for the guards to return. He was very worried. What can I do now? he thought. I must go to London. I must tell the D.O. that everything is all right on Doriphoros. If I don't, DOT will destroy mankind.

Carstairs looked at the computer. There were names and lights everywhere: Outpost Number 4—Skinner Group. Outpost Number 10—Le Roy Group, etc. He looked at the machine carefully. Perhaps there's a switch somewhere, he thought. Perhaps I can turn off the computer. Carstairs looked everywhere, but there weren't any switches.

Perhaps there's a switch somewhere, he thought.

It was like a big typewriter.

Carstairs went towards the eye in the centre of the computer.
It was black now because it wasn't flashing. He looked into
it, but he couldn't see anything.

Then he began to walk up and down. Suddenly, he noticed
something at one end of the room. It was like a big typewriter.
He went towards it quickly.

Carstairs stood beside the "typewriter". There were numbers
and letters on the keyboard. Then he looked back at the glass
eye. The red beam came on and the voice said: "This is the
Master. Guards 8732 and 8733, Skinner's Group, return to
Ante-Chamber." The light went out again. At once the numbers
8732 and 8733 moved on the keyboard of the "typewriter".

Carstairs looked at the keys carefully. It's only a typewriter,
he thought. The Master gives an order and then the keyboard
works. It sends messages all over the island. Now it has
sent a message to the guards. They will return soon. Suddenly,
Carstairs noticed something above the keyboard. He looked at
it carefully.

There were three words above the keyboard. The letters were small and Carstairs didn't notice them before. The three words were: CODE DIALLING SYSTEM.

Of course, Carstairs thought. This "typewriter" is really a code dialling system. All the guards have code numbers. I have a code number now! I am Number One! When the Master wants someone, it dials the code number and the guard gets the message. This "typewriter" controls the island.

Carstairs looked at his watch. The guards will be here soon, he thought and he walked away from the keyboard. As he walked, he repeated the words "Code Dialling System" to himself. Suddenly, he stopped. He said the three words very slowly and softly to himself: CODE—DIALLING—SYSTEM. Of course! he thought. CDS, *Code Dialling System*. What was that number the D.O. gave me in London? I learnt it, but can I remember it? CDS 4964 ... No! Carstairs put his hands over his eyes and thought hard. CDS 4967 ... That's it! I must remember it now. CDS 4967543287043789076543.

The three words were: CODE DIALLING SYSTEM.

53

He stood above the keyboard and touched the keys.

I've got nothing to lose, Carstairs thought. It's my only chance. He walked back to the "typewriter". He didn't walk too quickly. Then he stood above the keyboard and touched the keys. First he touched the letters "CDS".

The light came on. The red eye flashed angrily. "This is the Master," the voice said. "Number One, Carstairs. Do not touch Code Dialling System. Do not touch Code Dialling System." The voice was not deep and soft. It was sharp and angry—almost like Hardbaker's. "I am the Master! I am the Master!"

Carstairs touched the numbers 496754. He tried hard to remember the other numbers. The voice was very sharp now, but it wasn't clear. "I . . . am . . . the . . . Master . . ." it said. Carstairs touched the numbers 3287043. The voice broke. "I . . . I . . . am . . . the . . ." it said. Carstairs touched the numbers 789076543. "The Ma . . ." the voice said and stopped. It didn't continue. The red eye went out. Carstairs heard loud electronic bleeps and lights on the computer flashed, but the big glass eye was black and the voice remained silent.

Carstairs left the Control Room and went into the Ante-Chamber. He shut the door of the Control Room carefully. He looked round the Ante-Chamber. Everything was quiet. Hardbaker's dead body lay on the floor. The red light on the wall was out. The voice was silent.

Just then the two guards in silver suits appeared. They were very friendly now. "We are ready, Number One," they said. "The motor-boat is ready to leave. The captain is waiting."

"Thank you, guards," Carstairs said. "Take me to the boat." Carstairs followed the guards out of the building and they all went towards the sandy bay. They climbed down the rocks together. Carstairs saw the letters "EAS" on the rocks, but the "Enemy Alert System" wasn't flashing now.

I've stopped the computer, Carstairs thought. I've stopped DOT. He couldn't believe it. He laughed to himself as he climbed down the rocks. The motor-boat was waiting in the bay. Carstairs climbed on to it. There was no Death Capsule there now! Soon he was travelling across the blue Aegean.

Soon he was travelling across the blue Aegean.

He took a taxi.

Chapter 12   The Master of Magic

That evening Carstairs arrived at London Airport. It was fine
and warm in London. The sky was clear. Carstairs bought an
evening paper. He put it under his arm and left the Airport.
He took a taxi and was soon on his way to Headquarters. He
was in London again. He couldn't believe it. Was it really
true? He looked out of the window. Grey buildings flashed
past him. All the cars and buses were on the left of the road.
Yes! It really was true! He really was in London again. He
could see big red London buses. He was sitting in the back
of a black London taxi. He was travelling quickly towards
Headquarters. Everything was familiar—yet only this morning
... Carstairs shut his eyes and thought of the past four days.
So much has happened, he thought, but here in London
nothing has changed. The taxi stopped at some lights and
Carstairs opened his eyes. The paper was on his knees and he
looked down at it. Some words on the front page caught his
eye: COMPUTERS—DRAMATIC NEWS.

Carstairs read the newspaper story quickly.

"COMPUTERS—DRAMATIC NEWS

"We have just received dramatic reports from all over the world. Computers everywhere are working again. About 30,000 computers were out of order. Scientists couldn't understand why. At about midday today, computers suddenly started to work and scientists still can't explain it. We have received reports from the U.S.A., from the U.S.S.R. and from a lot of other countries. Over 1200 computers in Great Britain are now working again. 'It's like magic,' the scientists say. 'We can't explain it.'

"'This was a terribly serious problem,' said the Director of NASA. 'We had to stop our space programme. Our computers were stopping every minute. We couldn't work without them. Computers take men to the moon and planets and bring them back. Men can't travel in space without their help.'

"Something seems to be wrong with the world's biggest computer, D.O.T., on Doriphoros. At about midday…"

Carstairs read the newspaper story quickly.

"It's good to see you, John."

Carstairs didn't finish the story. He smiled to himself. Just then, the taxi stopped at H.Q. and he got out. He rang the bell and waited. An old man with grey hair opened the heavy door. "Oh, it's you, sir," the man said. "Director of Operations is expecting you. Please go straight upstairs."

"Thanks, Harry," Carstairs said. Carstairs went up and knocked at the door. The D.O. didn't say, "Come in," he got up and opened the door himself. He smiled when he saw Carstairs and shook his hand warmly. "It's good to see you, John," he said. "Come in and sit down."

Soon the D.O. and Carstairs were talking about "Operation Mastermind". Carstairs told the D.O. the story: how he swam to the island from the submarine; about the guards in their silver suits; about the Enemy Alert System; about Hardbaker; about the Death Capsule, and then ... about DOT. "I don't work for you, D.O.," Carstairs said. "Now I'm Number One, Carstairs, Agent of D.O.T." Carstairs copied DOT's deep jerky voice. "I am the Master," he said and the D.O. laughed.

Then Carstairs spoke seriously. "I still don't understand quite a lot of things, D.O.," he said. "Who was Hardbaker? Who was Professor Mastermind? How did he know this CDS number? CDS 4967543287043789076543. I'll never forget it now."

"I'll explain, John," the D.O. said "Five years ago the American Government sent two very clever computer engineers to Doriphoros. One of them was English and his name was Tom Smith. The other was American and his name was Rudolph P. Hardbaker. They both built this wonderful computer. Hardbaker was in charge, but he wanted more power. He quarrelled with Smith and two years ago Smith left the island and returned to London.

"Hardbaker wanted to control the world. But the computer wanted to control the world, too. The computer was soon in charge of the island, but it was afraid of Hardbaker and Smith. They both knew the CDS number and could destroy D.O.T. at any time. D.O.T. knew this and killed them both.

"Smith worked quietly in London as 'Professor Mastermind'.

"I'll explain, John," the D.O. said.

59

"Yes, Master," Carstairs said in a jerky voice.

"Smith liked his work as 'The Master of Magic' and he never wanted to work as a computer engineer again. But he read the reports about computers and was very worried. He came to our H.Q. and gave us the CDS number. The next day one of D.O.T.'s agents murdered him in that London theatre.

"D.O.T. really was the Master. Everyone on the island was afraid of the machine. The machine gave orders—and people acted. Even Hardbaker...even *you*, John!"

"Yes," Carstairs said. "When DOT spoke to me, I said, 'Yes, Master...'" Carstairs remembered the red glass eye!

"Now I have some work for you, John," the D.O. said. His face was very serious and he gave Carstairs an envelope. "Your orders are in this envelope," the D.O. said.

"But, D.O.," Carstairs cried. He was angry. He opened the envelope quickly. Then he smiled. Inside it there was a train ticket to Devon and a reservation at a small hotel.

"Now I'm rather busy," the D.O. said and smiled.

"Yes, Master," Carstairs said in a jerky voice and smiled too!

Exercises

1. Complete these questions. Use a question word from this list: *How?*
   How long? How long ago? How many? Who? What? Where? Which? Why?

   (a) ... did the great Memory Trick? Professor Mastermind.
   (b) ... was the number? 4967.
   (c) ... did Carstairs read his paper? In Leicester Square.
   (d) ... island did Carstairs visit? Doriphoros.
   (e) ... did he work in the theatre? Two years.
   (f) ... did he come to London? Two years ago.
   (g) ... computers are out of order? 25,000.
   (h) ... did he cut the box in two? With a saw.
   (i) ... did he feel hot? Because it was very warm in the theatre.
   (j) ... helped the Professor? A lady in the audience.

2. Complete these sentences. Use a preposition from this list: *by, out,*
   over, on, in, for, at, to, into, about, of, up, without, with.

   (a) Carstairs walked ... Waterloo Bridge.
   (b) He was ... his way to Headquarters.
   (c) I'll sit ... a public square and read a paper.
   (d) One thousand computers are now ... of order.
   (e) Carstairs walked ... twenty minutes.
   (f) I'm not ... a hurry.
   (g) You will travel ... plane.
   (h) A car will meet you ... Corfu Airport.
   (i) What's the name of the man ... charge?
   (j) Have you seen this story ... Professor Mastermind?
   (k) I have a map ....the island.
   (l) There weren't any lights ... all.
   (m) A large rock fell ... the water.
   (n) They were made ... heavy black rubber.
   (o) He picked ... a big rock.
   (p) I mustn't talk ... any guards.
   (q) It was a square building ... windows.
   (r) We must wait ... information.
   (s) What has happened ... all the other guards?
   (t) An old man ... grey hair opened the door.

3. Look at this example:

   > He was in London again. He was glad.
   > He was glad to be in London again.

   Now join these sentences in the same way.

   (a) He left London. He was sorry.
   (b) He met the D.O. He was pleased.
   (c) He saw me. He was glad.
   (d) He heard the news. He was surprised.
   (e) He was home again. He was happy.

4. Look at this example:

> I shall finish this trick. I shall go home.
> When I finish this trick, I shall go home.

Now join each of these sentences with *When*.

(a) I shall go home. I shall go to bed.
(b) He will find this. He will be angry.
(c) Carstairs will come back. He will have a holiday.
(d) The door will open. Carstairs will go inside.
(e) I shall be tired. I shall go to bed.

5. Look at this example:

> It's strange . . .
> It's strange, *isn't it?*

Complete these sentences.

(a) He has a map . . .
(b) It was easy to swim to the island . . .
(c) He walked through the water . . .
(d) He looks like a spaceman . . .
(e) They have found the body . . .
(f) He could see the island . . .
(g) He's a Secret Agent . . .
(h) He will be dead soon . . .
(i) He must get out . . .
(j) They can see a picture on the screen . . .

6. Give the past of the verbs in brackets, then look at page 2 of the story and check your answers:

A young man in the audience (get) up from his seat and (go) on to the stage. He (give) his watch to Professor Mastermind and the compère (leave) the stage. The Professor (take) a small hammer out of his pocket and (break) the watch to pieces. The young man (look) at his watch sadly. "It's all right," the Professor (smile). Then he (put) the pieces in a handkerchief. He (throw) the handkerchief into the air and (catch) it. When he (open) it, the watch (be) inside. It (be) all in one piece! The young man (be) glad. He (take) his watch quickly. Then he (sit) down while the audience (clap) loudly.

7. Add the missing punctuation in this conversation, then look at page 23 of the story and check your answer:

Are you from Number 10 Outpost the guard asked.
Carstairs shook his head. Number 4 Outpost he said.
Number 4 the guard said. What's your number
Number 4 Carstairs repeated.
No the man said not your Outpost Number. Your *number*.